Introducing
the New Lectionary

Getting the Bible into Worship

Michael Vasey

Tutor in Liturgy, St John's College, Durham

Jane Sinclair

Precentor, Sheffield Cathedral

Trevor Lloyd

Archdeacon of Barnstaple

Peter Moger

Precentor, Ely Cathedral

GROVE BOOKS LIMITED
RIDLEY HALL RD CAMBRIDGE CB3 9HU

Contents

The Cover Illustration is by Peter Ashton

First Impression July 1997
ISSN 0144-1728
ISBN 1 85174 349 9

1

Better Than Trainspotting
Michael Vasey

On November 30th 1997 a new calendar and lectionary, with attached collects and post-communion prayers, becomes a lawful option in the Church of England. The publication in June 1997 of this calendar and lectionary in three different forms, each with striking blue and yellow covers, marks not only the return of red rubrics to the liturgical books of the Church of England but also the first concrete manifestation to many ordinary Anglicans that 'a new generation of liturgy' is on its way.

A New Generation of Liturgy

There are many signs that worship is alive and well in Britain. New worship songs appear every day. 'Postmodernism' and a new celebration of cultural pluralism mean that there is space in the public imagination for the re-emergence of corporate spiritualities. The old confidence of many strands of Christian belief that faith needs to be expressed primarily in the head ('theology'), in the heart and in personal morality is breaking down. The realities of life and the academic disciplines of sociology are making it clear that faith must be expressed publicly and corporately if it is to be real. Worship is not just an emotional release for the inadequate or a crutch for those left in a cultural time-warp, it is the primary place where people meet God and where their faith is formed and nurtured.

Although worship is very much alive and many Christian groups and congregations are busy finding ways to embody their faith, fewer people see the ancient wisdom of the church as a resource. Much Anglican leadership is alienated from liturgy, protecting the forms they know—*ASB* or *BCP*—but having little real understanding of, or sympathy for, the enterprise. If the new generation of liturgy takes much of the Church of England by surprise, the main reason will be that no resources have been made available for communication or education in liturgy.

While some regarded the *ASB* as a one step modernization—replacing one Ford Escort by another—it was always more accurate to see it as an important transition stage into a different worship culture—more like moving from a typewriter to an early personal computer.[1] Although the *Book of Common Prayer* continued much of the old wisdom of the Western church it was profoundly shaped by two cultural features of the sixteenth century: the invention of printing and a single national authority legislating for nation and church. *ASB* began a change

---

1   cf 'Have they gone mad?' pp 3-7, *Introducing Patterns for Worship* by Trevor Lloyd, Jane Sinclair, Michael Vasey (Grove Worship Series No 111, Nottingham: Grove Books, 1990)

back to seeing worship as a corporate act with a clear shape with variable prayers being fitted into a framework. It made important strides towards recovering a unitive liturgy for the Church of England and towards discovering a style appropriate to the modern gathered congregation of between 20 and 300 people.

While many have thought the 'new' Ford Escort would do, and the upheaval of change not worth the fuss, successive Liturgical Commissions have been following through the logic of *ASB*'s attempt to renew the Church's worship. *Lent, Holy Week Easter* (1986) and *The Promise of His Glory* (1989, 1991) extended the resource book approach as well as making available more seasonal material. *Patterns for Worship* (1989, 1995), in providing for occasions when more flexibility was required, made a number of important advances. It gave guidance on how to put an act of worship together and do justice to shape and flow; it moved firmly from a legal to a pastoral and educational approach to liturgy; and it returned to the pre-print understanding of the liturgical book as liturgical manual rather than script for each pew member. Two important reports set out the philosophy that would govern the new generation of liturgy: *The Renewal of Common Prayer* (ed Michael Perham, 1993) proposed that the unity of Church of England worship should be seen not in fixed texts enforced by law but in an 'evolving core' sustained by a balance of publication, education and regulation. *On The Way: Towards an Integrated Approach to Christian Initiation* (House of Bishops, 1995) identifies the importance of reintegrating mission, liturgy, education, and spirituality.

In July 1994 the House of Bishops invited the General Synod to agree an overall plan for Church of England worship beyond 2000. A composite motion was adopted which, together with motions adopted in the 1991 debates on Christian initiation, has provided the framework in which Liturgical Commission and General Synod are working.[2] Broadly the plan is to replace the bulky *ASB* in 2001 by a smaller 'pew' book including the main modern and traditional language services in use on Sundays, a personal prayer book, and a small number of resource books for those who plan and lead worship. In 1996 the Standing Committee of General Synod established a Liturgical Publications Group, chaired by the Bishop of Guildford, to oversee the publication of the new material—both in book form and in forms that can be used with personal computers. This group has in turn set up a Communication and Education sub-group chaired by Trevor Lloyd which is working with PRAXIS to implement an overall educational strategy.

Calendar and Lectionary

The Christian Year: Calendar, Lectionary and Collects (Church House Publishing, 1997) represents the first wave of this new generation of liturgy. At first sight this may seem an odd starting point. Many Christians will instinctively view the church calendar as high church flummery, a lectionary as a crutch for inadequate worship leaders who do not know their Bible, and a cycle of saints' days (*Sanctorale*)

---

2   This is set out in *Liturgical Revision 1995-2000*, GS Misc 459 (1995). An updated and more popularly presented version of this is due to be published later in 1997.

as absolutely off the wall—perhaps even a sign of the terminal irrelevance of Anglicanism in the modern world. An interest in lectionaries probably beats trainspotting as a conversational turn-off.

But calendar and lectionary are actually about the life-transforming encounter between Bible and church. Together they are the mechanics of how the Bible gets into the worship of the church. The church of Christ is enjoined to 'let the word of Christ dwell in you richly, teach and admonish one another in all wisdom, and sing psalms and hymns and spiritual songs in your hearts to God' (Col 3.16) and 'to attend to the public reading of Scripture' (1 Tim 4.13). The first finds its outworking in calendar (as well as liturgy); the second in lectionary. The restoration of public Bible reading and the reform of the calendar and lectionary were Cranmer's first priorities. The same priority has operated in the influential liturgical reforms in the Roman Catholic Church which were instigated by the Second Vatican Council.

Calendar and lectionary are turn-offs for many people not simply because they are complex subjects but because they lie so deep in the life of a community that we do not know that they are there. Every worshipping community has patterns of worship (liturgy) and principles that govern how the Bible is read (lectionary). Reviewing or reforming them is like learning not to pollute the environment; the biggest battle is to realize that the way things are is not simply a given but is part of a shared life commitment. This is even more the case for the public ordering of time—for calendar.

a) Calendar

Intrinsic to any community is the way it orders its time, its calendar; calendars are not neutral or simply 'scientific'; they embody the theology that holds the community together. The way a community orders its time is shaped by four factors: the way it finds its livelihood within the creation; the God it worships—what it acknowledges as reality; the symbols that give it coherence; and the technology by which it measures time. This can be seen clearly in the attention that the Old Testament gives to calendar (see Leviticus 23; Exodus 23.14-17). It is equally present in the dispersed and mobile Christian communities of the New Testament with their focus on 'the first day of the week'—the memorial of the resurrection, with the link between Lord's Day and Lord's Supper, and with a continuing dialogue with the Old Testament festivals of Passover and Pentecost (see 1 Cor 5.7; Acts 2.1, 20.16; 1 Cor 16.8).

The deregulation of Sunday trading is confronting evangelical Christians with the theological nature of calendar, although there is not as yet much evidence of reflection, probably because evangelicals think more easily in terms of function rather than symbol. It is becoming clearer that the modern secular calendar is not neutral. It is created by the society's view of ultimate reality and by the technology by which it measures time.[3] Christians are part of the world as well as owing

---

3   On the influence of technology see chapter 4 of Susan J White. *Christian Worship and Technological Change* (Nashville: Abingdon Press, 1994).

a different allegiance within it. Questions of calendar are integral to mission and identity.

If evangelicals are often inadvertent secularists, 'Catholics' often fall into the opposite error of treating the calendar as simply a historic given of the faith—the expression of an unchanging (and past) reality. But the church is part of the world and its ordering of its time has to be seen as dynamically related to its social context—as a conscious symbolic dialogue with a present reality in which God is actively present. There was some recognition of this in *The Promise of His Glory* in its anthology approach and in the introduction to the proposed Lectionary 2: 'The length of the festival seasons has varied in different parts of the Church. It may be that the preferred length of a season is partly determined by social factors' (p 377).

The Christian calendar as we know it, and as it finds expression in the new Church of England provision, emerged in conscious dialogue with societies that were serving other gods. Although properly celebrated with art and song and characterized by strange solemnity and light-hearted festivity, it needs to be seen as serious—as one of the most profound expressions of Christian mission. Out of this continuing dialogue the Christian calendar has three interwoven elements:[4]

1. A cycle of festivals generated by the death and resurrection of Christ. The heart of the cycle is the celebration of the death and resurrection from Holy Saturday to Easter morning and the keeping of a fifty day celebration of the new creation between Easter and Pentecost. Other features of the cycle like Palm Sunday, Good Friday, Ascension Day and the season of Lent emerged as part of the church's engagement with Mediterranean urban culture.

2. A cycle of festivals generated by the incarnation that runs from the Feast of the Annunciation through Advent, Christmas and Epiphany to the Feast of the Presentation of Christ on the 2nd February. The date of March 25 for the Annunciation was arrived at by reference to the supposed date of Jesus' death around Easter: a perfect man living a perfect period of time.

3. A cycle of saints days. This arose from local Christian communities keeping the anniversary of local martyrs and generated a complex system expressing the reality of the other world, the character and cost of Christian witness (Greek: *martyria*), and the common participation of the church in the new creation.

b) Lectionary.

Public reading is alien to our culture and so is often passed over or taken for granted. Easy rhetoric about Word and Sacrament mean that 'Word' is often understood simply as preaching. However, the Anglican Reformers and Richard

---

4   The most useful summary of the scholarship underlying current calendrical reform can be found in pp 125-142 of Thomas Talley, *Worship: Reforming Tradition* (Washington: Pastoral Press, 1990). Important and accessible are Michael Perham and Kenneth Stevenson's, *Welcoming the Risen Christ* (SPCK, 1986) and *Waiting for the Coming Christ* (SPCK, 1991).

Hooker were clear that the ordered public reading of Scripture was theologically prior to, and the proper context for, preaching. Because dispute in the Church of England has focused mainly on the interpretation of the eucharist, little thought has been given to the other central ritual act of the church's weekly worship, the public reading of Scripture.[5]

The Scriptures themselves are in origin a collection of hand-written texts designed, either by original intent or by inclusion within the canon, to be heard by the gathered people of God. This corporate reception in the Christian assembly—and its priority over private Bible-reading—is important to the proper interpretation of Scripture.

How the public reading of Scripture is arranged and ordered has to reflect both the nature of the church—a dispersed people focused on Christ and the kingdom of God—and the nature of Scripture—a varied collection of books, cohering around Jesus and the central themes of the unfolding history of God's salvation. Historically lectionaries—in the sense of the ordered selection of Bible passages—have been generated by two different and complementary approaches:

1. An arrangement of seasonal or thematic readings related to the great corporate celebrations of the Christian calendar. This has covered not only the festivals themselves but also the periods of preparation that we now know as Advent and Lent.
2. The continuous or semi-continuous reading of books of the Bible in ways governed by local tradition and choice—'local' here referring here primarily to the community of Christians in a city gathered around a bishop. Although this pattern was often related to preaching, there was regularly more than one reading at any liturgical assembly.

At the same time the custom became established that the reading of Scripture at the eucharist finished with a reading from one of the Gospels to embody the expectation that it is Christ who speaks to the church through all the Scriptures. In time the two approaches to lectionary were fused together into the overarching Bible reading schemes that are found in the lectionaries of the 'liturgical' churches.

In the liturgical reforms of the 1960s two different approaches to the reform of the lectionary emerged.[6] The Joint Liturgical Group's proposal, effectively adopted in *ASB*, attempted to give the whole year a Trinitarian shape with three readings each Sunday linked by a theme. With its *Lectionary for Mass* the Roman Catholic

5   I have attempted to explore this subject at greater length in *Reading the Bible at the Eucharist* (Grove Worship Series No 94, Nottingham: Grove Books, 1986) and in 'Scripture and Prayer: Enriching the Revised Roman Missal.' *Liturgy*, December 1994/January 1995, Vol 19.2, pp 57-71. See also 'Scripture and Eucharist' in the forthcoming collection of essays edited by David Holeton arising from the 1995 International Anglican Liturgical Consultation at Dublin. Note also Stephen Sykes' useful essay on 'The Anglican Character' in *Celebrating the Anglican Way*, Ian Bunting (Ed), (Hodder & Stoughton, 1996) pp 21-32.

6   It is clear that there was some interaction between the two developments—see Annibale Bugnini, *The Reform of the Liturgy 1948-1975* (Minnesota: The Liturgical Press, ET, 1990) p 416, and Donald Gray, *Ronald Jasper* (SPCK, 1997) pp 84-5.

Church preserved the distinction between a seasonal and non-seasonal approach to the lectionary. The result was a three-year lectionary, part of which is organized around the two cycles mentioned above, but with the rest of the year—what came to be called 'ordinary time'—committed to semi-continuous reading through the gospels and apostolic writings (a more accurate term than the common Anglican term 'epistles').[7]

The approach of the Roman Catholic three-year lectionary proved attractive to other churches in the USA and Canada, so that the North American Churches, through an ecumenical body called the Consultation on Common Texts (CCT), produced a variant on this lectionary called the *Common Lectionary* (1983). The most controversial features of the Roman Catholic three-year lectionary turned out to be its tendency to 'fillet' Bible passages for the sake of brevity and its typological use of the Old Testament in ordinary time. This latter feature was strongly criticized by black churches and other traditions who valued the narrative material of the Old Testament in its own right. The 1983 *Common Lectionary* therefore replaced the Roman Catholic OT readings in ordinary time with semi-continuous readings—focusing on the Pentateuch in the year of Matthew, the period of the monarchy in the year of Mark, and prophets and wisdom in the year of Luke. This was in turn criticized by others as a move to 'soap opera' lectionary.

The *Revised Common Lectionary* (RCL) was finally published in 1992 as the fruit of further discussion.[8] The British Joint Liturgical Group, whose then Chairman Donald Gray had been involved with ELLC in revising the *Common Lectionary*, then added its endorsement to RCL thus effectively sinking its own alternative four-year lectionary *JLG2*. RCL dealt with the question of the Old Testament by including both tracks and also incorporated various other changes. It is in the process of being adopted by all the historic British denominations apart from the Roman Catholic Church and the Baptist Union. Interest in the RCL is being expressed in other language groups and discussions continue with the Vatican as to whether its use might be permitted to Roman Catholics. It has been taken as the basis for the new provision in the Church of England.

The idea of a fixed lectionary may come as a surprise to many evangelical Anglicans who are accustomed to ignoring the requirements of the lectionary, confident—perhaps overconfident?—that they could do justice on their own to the breadth and balance of Scripture. The original report (GS1161) from the Liturgical Commission, debated in General Synod in July 1995, followed *The Promise of*

---

7   The *Ordo Lectionum Missae* was published in 1969. Its opening 'Instruction,' as with all Roman Catholic documents, is a very clear and informative introduction to the lectionary. An interesting article by Eileen Schuller 'Some Criteria for the Choice of Scripture Texts in the Roman Lectionary' pp 385-404 in *Shaping English Liturgy* by Peter C Finn and James M Schellman (Eds), analyses the reasoning behind the omission of so called difficult texts in the OLM. These intentional omissions include some of the miracle stories in Acts and the reference to Ebed-melech as a 'eunuch' in Jeremiah 38!

8   Canterbury Press, 1992. (This includes, on pp 77-9, a useful account of changes to the 1983 lectionary). 'The Ecumenical Import of Lectionary Reform' by Horace T Allen, Jr in *Shaping English Liturgy* (pp 361-384) gives a more extended discussion of the whole development.

His Glory in proposing the use of authorized lectionary 'packages' and other departures from the lectionary except from Advent 3 to Epiphany 1 and from Palm Sunday to Trinity Sunday. The Revision Committee took the view that such departures would tend to undermine the new lectionary and proposed to limit them to ordinary time—February 3rd to Ash Wednesday, and Trinity 1 to the Sunday before Advent.

The Renewal of Preaching?

There are currently many signs of a renewed interest in preaching in the church. Mention could be made of the important work of the Proclamation Trust as well as the strong interest in homiletics in North America, often focusing on the importance of doing justice to the way in which Scripture communicates.[9]

Many hope that the abandonment of the *ASB*'s thematic lectionary will help renew preaching. Certainly many who listen to preaching will be pleased to escape the intellectual game of anticipating how the preacher will find the theme in the passages. However, the shift back to a non-thematic lectionary may not, of itself, be enough. It is certainly possible to imagine a return to an endless string of pious reflections loosely attached to the Gospel reading of the day. Another danger brought out by Ian Bunting in his very fine Grove booklet *Preaching at Communion (i)* is that the liturgical context can lure the preacher into a cosy triumphalism which only looks forward to the reception of the sacrament rather than to the costly rigours and complexity of life in the world.

Part of the remedy may lie not only in learning from contemporary emphases on how Scripture communicates but also in making contact with past traditions of liturgical preaching. In his *Landmarks in the History of Preaching* (SPCK, 1950) Y Brillioth follows C Smyth in charting the transformation of authentic preaching after Lancelot Andrewes into 'a moral essay' and acclaiming Charles Simeon's importance in reclaiming a classic tradition of liturgical preaching.[10]

It will be important also to recover the liturgical character of preaching. Against the Puritans, the Anglican Reformers and their successors thought it important to set preaching within the context of the whole community's reception of Scripture. The preacher is not to be the sole repository of Christian knowledge or of the mind of God nor the main channel of communicating the Christian story. I once heard Oliver O'Donovan speak warmly of preaching in a setting where the Scriptures were experienced as 'the common possession of the people of God' and contrasting this with the Puritan idea of the preacher as prophet. Again preaching is more than teaching—more than passing on information. Much black preaching, for example, demonstrates that good preaching can itself be an expression of

---

9   See 'Preaching should be a speaking *of* Scripture and not *about* Scripture' in 'Interpretation and Preaching' David G Buttrick, *Interpretation* XXXV. 1. 1981 pp 46ff. *Resourcing the Word* an extensive bibliography on preaching. can be obtained for £5 from David Day. St John's College. Durham DH1 3RJ.

10 cf Hugh Evan Hopkins, *Charles Simeon: Preacher Extraordinary* (Grove Booklets on Liturgy No 18. Nottingham: Grove Books 1979). Note particularly Simeon's emphasis on doing justice to the mood or 'spirit' of a passage (p 8).

worship—as much response as proclamation and itself a liturgical expression of the people's praise and prayer.

Preaching cannot be a substitute for (or even the main means of) the church grounding itself in the Scriptures. The revival of preaching will require careful attention to how the community of faith makes the Scriptures its own. It will involve the recovery of an appropriate rhetoric, a greater honesty about life in the world, and a deeper shared engagement with Scripture on the part of both preacher and people. Getting the Bible back into worship through calendar and lectionary is an integral part of such a renewal.

2

The New Order
Michael Vasey

The new calendar, lectionary and collects for the Church of England have been published in three forms. A 'desk' version, *The Christian Year: Calendar, Lectionary and Collects*, includes the whole provision and also an edited version (pp 241-252) of the Commentary that was part of the Liturgical Commission's first report to General Synod. *The Christian Year Collects and Post Communion Prayers for Sundays and Festivals* is an 'altar book' designed for use by those who lead worship. *The Christian Year Advent 1997 to Advent 1998* simply extracts the Sunday provision for the period stated. All three are beautifully produced and attempt to break new ground in elegant and user-friendly liturgical publishing.

It is already clear that the new calendar and lectionary are going to make available considerable new resources for local congregations . On my desk lie *The Liturgy Planner*[11] aimed primarily at Roman Catholic parishes, *The New Handbook of the Christian Year* produced for North American Methodists[12] and *The Fullness of Time* with sermon summaries for every Gospel from Advent 1997 until the Millennium.[13] It is certain that there will be much more. The Commentary section in the full edition gives a very clear account of the principles and detail of the calendar and lectionary.[14] Both calendar and lectionary are best seen as riches to be explored at leisure. Simply as signposts in this exploration it may be worth picking out certain features of the new landscape.

---

11 Available from 30 North Terrace. Mildenhall. Suffolk IP28 7AB.
12 Hoyt L Hickman (Ed) et al. (Nashville: Abingdon Press. 1986. 1992).
13 Joseph Donders (CAFOD. 1996.1997).
14 It will be supplemented in September 1997 by Michael Perham's *Celebrating the Christian Story: An Introduction to the new Calendar, Lectionary and Collects* (SPCK).

- The Church Year returns to a clear beginning at Advent and to the *Book of Common Prayer*'s naming of Sundays after Trinity.
- Alongside the *RCL* readings for the 'Principal Service' there are readings for two other services. Those for the 'Third Service' also designed with a Sunday Office in mind and, in Ordinary Time, are the same each year.
- The minister is charged with 'ensuring that, in any year, a balance is maintained' between Old and New Testaments (p 36). It is 'unhelpful' to move between 'Continuous' and 'Related' tracks of Old Testament readings (p 37).
- An alternative table of psalmody is provided where the *RCL* choice seems too long (p 95).
- Departures from the lectionary in the limited open season are to be made only 'after due consultation with the Parochial Church Council' (p 36).
- As a weekday lectionary has yet to be offered, interim publications (such as the SPCK 1998 Almanac) may face problems in integrating old and new. Beware and be principled.
- The collects are no longer thematic in Ordinary Time but aim to continue the Anglican tradition of a 'prayer for the week.' They are often close to those in the *Book of Common Prayer* and were largely agreed with the other Anglican Provinces in Britain and Ireland.[15] (Two *Prayer Book* collects—Trinity 4 and Trinity 6—have been corrected on the ground that 'the *Prayer Book* version had mistranslated the Latin original and, in so doing, lost the force of the original').
- In the Sundays after Trinity, collects and lectionary de-couple as the only way of having collects for the week and using the *RCL* readings on the same Sunday as other churches.
- The longer endings to the collects may be omitted (p 118).
- As few as possible of the post-communion prayers begin 'Almighty God' so as to avoid triggering the congregational prayer of self-offering.
- GS1161 'did not rule out the possibility of 'Lectionary Prayers,' more likely provided by independent authors and publishers…, for those seeking a prayer that draws out the meaning from a particular lection' (p 23). Such prayers may appear with the planned new translation of the Roman Catholic Sacramentary.
- 'All Sundays celebrate the paschal mystery of the death and resurrection of the Lord' (p 10).
- Epiphany is seen as a season that concludes with the Presentation of Christ in the Temple—a rich biblical festival that provides a bridge between the two calendrical cycles, looking back to the incarnation and forward to the passion.
- The major change to *RCL* is the introduction of a Creation theme on the Second Sunday before Lent with appropriate readings in each of the three years. This corrects a weakness in *RCL* and resonates with Cranmer's reading of Genesis from Septuagesima.

---

15 But a unilateral change was made to the collect for St David's day!

- In Year A the very long readings from John on the 3rd, 4th and 5th Sundays of Lent are integrally related to prayer for candidates for baptism at Easter—watch this space.
- Easter is seen as a season celebrating the new creation with Sundays *of* Easter rather than *after* Easter. Two features may disconcert traditional Anglicans. The first is that readings from Acts replace the Old Testament. (For the weak there are OT alternatives on p 60). The second is that, as part of this reality, 'prayer and preparation to celebrate the outpouring of the Spirit' occurs on the days between Ascension and Pentecost rather than in the old 'octave' after Whitsun.
- All Saints Day may be celebrated on a Sunday and marks a shift of mood to the Sundays before Advent when the liturgical colour may change from green to red. (Earlier proposals to style these Sundays of the Kingdom were abandoned at the Revision stage.) The Sunday before Advent is styled Christ the King.
- 'Bible Sunday' moves from Advent 2 to being an optional provision, possibly for use on one of the Sundays in late October or early November. Cranmer's 'read, mark, learn' collect goes to the Last Sunday after Trinity.
- The *Sanctorale* distinguishes between Festivals (bold and red in the tables), Lesser Festivals which may be observed 'at the level appropriate to a particular church,' and Commemorations which are made, where appropriate, 'by a mention in prayers of intercession and thanksgiving.' In the case of Lesser Festivals and Commemorations limited and discerning selection is invited.[16]
- Optional collects are provided for Lesser Festivals. Possible lections are printed elsewhere (pp 111-116) to discourage overuse.
- The Revision Committee asserted the 'fifty year rule' for Commemorations as well as Lesser Festivals in the case of all but martyrs, so removing among others: Amy Carmichael, Michael Ramsey, John XXIII, C S Lewis, and Simon Kimbangu ('Evangelist and Witness in Zaire').
- Despite a desire to steer a number of Saint's days out of Lent, Edward King (8 March) and Cranmer (21 March) made it back. (In general there has been careful with Roman Catholic revision of the Sanctorale for England and Wales.)
- Africa, Asia and women are well represented among the Lesser Festivals and Commemorations.

---

16 Further provision of collects and readings and so on is to be published as *Exciting Holiness* (ed Brother Tristam, SSF) by Canterbury Press in September 1997.

3

Using the Calendar and Lectionary
Jane Sinclair

The new calendar and lectionary have been used on Sundays and festivals at Sheffield Cathedral since the autumn of 1993, with a 12-month break in 1994/5 when the Cathedral reverted to the *ASB* Sunday lectionary. The Cathedral's reasons for adopting the new calendar and lectionary were varied. Members of the regular congregations and preachers alike welcomed the richer spread of Scripture which the new lectionary affords. During 1994/5 many commented on how they found the reversion to the themed *ASB* Sunday lectionary comparatively restrictive in feel. Members of the Cathedral chapter and ecumenically-minded laity welcomed the ecumenical possibilities of the new provision. And the Cathedral's Precentor was happy to give the new lectionary and calendar a trial run on behalf of the Liturgical Commission. Overall, the Cathedral community has found the new provision to be stimulating, refreshing and accessible.

Experience of the new lectionary also suggests some opportunities to seize and some pitfalls that the busy worship leader would do well to avoid.

Opportunities
The new lectionary provides a three-year cycle of Scripture readings for three Sunday services. In most churches the 'principal service' provision will apply to the main Sunday act of worship (whether eucharistic or not). The 'second service' provision applies to the secondary act of Sunday worship such as Evensong, or the 8am service of Holy Communion. The 'third service' provision applies to any tertiary act of Sunday worship such as a said service of Morning or Evening Prayer or its equivalent. The Scripture readings are set in a semi-continuous pattern, each book being covered over a period of weeks. The synoptic gospels are each covered in turn during the three-year cycle, with St John's gospel shared between all three years. All this means that congregations and preachers alike are exposed to a much wider range of Scripture than they have been accustomed to under the two-year *ASB* Sunday lectionary. For example, in June and July of year C the second service lectionary enables a congregation to dwell on the book of Genesis for ten consecutive weeks. The narrative aspects of the Scripture are thereby highlighted, and regular attenders can expect to hear the main thrust of the stories of Abraham and his successors over a number of weeks. Similarly in July and August of year B the principal service lectionary enables a congregation to dwell on the letter to the Ephesians over seven consecutive weeks. The argument of the letter can be followed and preached week by week as the epistle is read.

Obviously this style of reading the Scriptures, whilst having much in common with the more or less continuous readings in the daily Morning and Evening

Prayer and Eucharistic lectionaries, is new to many Sunday congregations, and needs careful introduction to preachers and listeners alike. Preachers may need reassurance about their ability to handle a biblical text without the help of themes. They will certainly need to be warned against attempting to find links between the passages of Scripture set. With the exception of major festivals and feast days, and the two Sundays before Lent, the lectionary provision is not 'themed.' Readings run concurrently alongside one another, and are not chosen to match each other thematically. Instead, preachers need to plan in advance how they are to preach through a book. If more than one person regularly preaches in a church, some co-ordination will be needed to ensure consistency in the content of sermons. This is an obvious need if a church opts for the 'open season' modules outlined in note six of the new lectionary provision. What is less obvious is that forward planning is also needed in relation to the regular lectionary provision as well.

In order to help regular members of the congregation to make the most of the semi-continuous nature of the readings, it is particularly important to preach one or two sermons giving an overview of a book and its significance when embarking on a new biblical book. This is particularly true in Advent, when the principal lectionary embarks on a new Gospel of the year. In addition, at Sheffield Cathedral the experience of the new lectionary has prompted regular meetings of those licensed to preach in the Cathedral to review the forms and styles of preaching, and to discuss issues of hermeneutics and application. Whilst demanding, this has and is proving to be a valuable learning exercise for all who preach regularly, no matter how experienced they are at preaching.

The question of choices to be made between lectionary options is one that appears under several guises in the new lectionary provision. In the first instance, there are occasional choices to be made between different sets of readings on particular days. On Principal Feasts, Principal Holy Days and Festivals, the lections in all three years are generally very familiar, and entirely what the preacher and congregation might expect. At Christmas and Easter it is perfectly possible, with judicious choices, to have lections which exactly match those in the *ASB* or those in the *Book of Common Prayer* if the incumbent so wishes. However, the choice of lectionary provision on Principal Feasts does require careful forward planning if the accidental repetition of readings is to be avoided.

In the summer and autumn months, there are two options in the Old Testament lections. At the principal Sunday service, one lectionary stream allows the church to continue the semi-continuous reading of Scripture, whilst a second allows the church to follow a series of Old Testament readings which are typologically related to the gospel reading of the day, and are not semi-continuous. Thus in Year B the Sundays in October allow for semi-continuous readings from the book of Job *or* offers an alternative series of readings drawn from Genesis, Amos, Isaiah and Jeremiah. The important point is that the choice ought to be made consciously at least at the beginning of the lectionary year. or preferably at the beginning of any three-year lectionary cycle.

In the calendar, the change which is most immediate and striking is the reversion to the *Book of Common Prayer* nomenclature for Sundays after Trinity. This helps to underline the centrality of the Holy Trinity to the basic doctrine of the Church, doctrine which distinguishes the Christian community from other faith communities, and avoids the pitfall of having two Sunday titles differing by one digit in churches where the *BCP* and the *ASB* are used cheek by jowl.

The calendar as a whole is very conservative in feel, with few surprises at the level of Principal Feasts, Principal Holy Days or Festivals. The Presentation of Christ in the Temple has become a Principal Feast, reflecting its key pivotal position in the Christian year as the Church turns from Christmas towards the Passion. Other Principal Feasts remain unchanged.

Of the Festivals it is worth noting that George (23 April) and the Visitation (31 May) now appear as Festivals as opposed to their Lesser Festival categorization in the *ASB*. Christ the King (the Sunday next before Advent) appears in the calendar officially as a Festival for the first time; and the principal feast of the Blessed Virgin Mary has been shifted from September 8 to August 15. The collects and lections for the Blessed Virgin Mary are careful to reflect doctrinal statements about the Blessed Virgin Mary which are acceptable across the breadth of tradition in the Church of England.

The lectionary and calendar provision is supplemented by a rich selection of collects of the day and post-communion collects. To members of congregations who know or remember the *Book of Common Prayer*, some of these collects will have strong resonances in their language and rhythms. To others unfamiliar with the *Book of Common Prayer*, the collects may sometimes sound 'weightier' than their *ASB* counterparts. Many of the post-communion collects are brand-new compositions.

Pitfalls to Avoid

For all the opportunities which the new provision affords, there are a number of pitfalls which those new to the calendar and lectionary would do well to avoid.

The new Sunday lectionary provision for the principal, second and third services sometimes sits ill with the current *ASB* daily office lectionary for Morning and Evening Prayer and Communion. Unfortunate repetitions of readings can and do occur from time to time. Make an uninformed choice of readings in the year B principal lectionary for July and you can find yourself reading 2 Samuel on Sundays and on weekdays for a number of weeks, with irritating consequences.

More problematic is how to handle the period from the Friday after Ascension Day until the Saturday after the day of Pentecost inclusive. In the new calendar the nine days between the Friday after Ascension Day and the eve of Pentecost are a period of prayer for the coming of the Holy Spirit, the liturgical colour is red, and the daily readings ought to reflect pneumatic themes. On the day after Pentecost the new calendar and lectionary revert firmly to 'ordinary time.' However, the *ASB* daily lectionary provision avoids reference to the coming of the Holy Spirit until Pentecost itself, and then sets daily readings on the theme of the Spirit for the days between Pentecost and Trinity Sunday. The Liturgical Commission and the General Synod will presumably now address the need to revise the daily lectionary. In the meanwhile, some careful and creative reordering of daily lectionary provision around Ascensiontide and Pentecost is needed if sense is to be made of the new calendar and lectionary.

It is also the case that whilst the new calendar solves the *ASB/Prayer Book* problem of dual-titles Sundays after Pentecost/Trinity, it creates a parallel difficulty with the Sundays of Eastertide. In the *Prayer Book* and *ASB* the Sundays after Easter Day are titled 'Sundays after Easter,' the first Sunday after Easter being the Sunday popularly called 'Low Sunday.' The new calendar is more theologically and liturgically consistent, titling the Sundays after Easter Day 'Sundays of Easter.' Thus Easter Day is the first Sunday of Easter, and 'Low Sunday' is titled 'The Second Sunday of Easter.' Consequently, if a church uses both the *Book of Common Prayer* and the new calendar, the Sundays of/after Easter are going to be out of digital synchronization with each other. In order to lessen confusion at Sheffield Cathedral it was decided to use the new calendar's titles, 'Sundays of Easter' on all printed materials, and as and when necessary to indicate verbally on what page the *Prayer Book* collect of the day and lections were to be found.

There is one further issue of forward planning with the lectionary which has to be borne in mind by churches which use only two readings at the principal Sunday service. For a principal service which is Holy Communion and at which only two readings are read, choices have to be made about whether and when to opt for a sequence of Old Testament readings or for a sequence of New Testament readings to accompany the gospel reading. The simplest solution is to opt for Old Testament readings for one year and New Testament readings for the next year. By alternating year by year, all the Old Testament and New Testament readings will be read at the principal service over the course of six years. This pattern clearly requires a long-term view of lectionary planning for a local church.

Conclusion

It is well worth becoming familiar with the new calendar and lectionary. In practice, the new provision is not nearly as complex to use as it might seem on first acquaintance. Approached with imagination and good sense, the provision allows for the reading and hearing of a wide and rich range of Scripture within a Church year which ensures that the fullness of the gospel is proclaimed and experienced by the Church. The worst potential pitfalls of the temporary parallel use of *ASB* daily lectionary provision and the new Sunday provision can be avoided, and the potential advantages of the 'open season' lectionary modules and the semi-continuous reading of Scripture in the regular lectionary provision can all be maximized with careful forward planning. Plenty of helpful, accessible and easy to use documentation is being made available to aid clergy and other worship leaders to use the lectionary and calendar to their best advantage. If the use of a common lectionary among the mainstream Christian Churches helps to draw us together in closer unity around the Word of God, that is only to the benefit of the proclamation of the gospel.

4

Putting Services Together with the New Lectionary
Trevor Lloyd

At first sight it may seem very much easier to put together services such as Rite A Holy Communion or a Family Service from *A Service of the Word* with a thematic lectionary rather than a non-thematic one, and the change from the thematic *ASB* to the non-thematic new lectionary may be viewed with some apprehension by many people. It certainly requires a different approach. There is no possibility of going around the same basic syllabus every two years, raking over the ideas which went into a service the year before last. Instead, the door is wide open to a new kind of adventure in which the two or three readings play on one another like parts of a kaleidoscope, and in which the theme for the service can emerge from any one of the readings, and is capable of more variation from year to year. The whole approach is new and demands a different kind of picture in the mind. Throw out the old static picture of the leader as a teacher with a syllabus to present ('Today's lesson/theme is…') and take on a moving image of the church gathered around the Scriptures, engaging with the retelling of the story from week to week.

The arrival of a new lectionary gives the kind of impetus some churches will need to reconsider how services are constructed, what elements are important, what can be changed and varied, and what needs to stick with tradition. Perhaps the PCC should have a discussion about this whole area with an agenda which might include some of these items:

- An introduction to the new lectionary using the ideas in the introduction to *Calendar, Lectionary and Collects* and in this booklet.
- How the new lectionary will affect the teaching programme of the church.
- How the new lectionary will affect the way in which services are put together, with some input from those responsible for music, drama, children and young people.
- Whether the lectionary readings should be advertised the week before, for example on the church notice sheet (if there is one), to emphasize the continuity of the readings and to help everyone prepare.
- Whether there is a need for training people more widely in the reading and 'performing' of the Scriptures in the service.

Some Steps Towards Putting the Service Together
Those involved need to understand how the lectionary works. If possible, read the introduction to the main volume, together with a commentary such as this. Get some feel for the whole year which is devoted to one of the three synoptic

gospels, and then look at what season of the year the Sunday for which you are planning falls in, and see how the pattern of the other readings works for that time of year.

Look at the readings over a period of four to six weeks around the service for which you are planning. This is important as the readings no longer focus on a separate theme for each Sunday, but are part of an on-going story. Look for the links.

Decide if those who are planning the worship and responsible for the preaching are going to stick with a particular book for several weeks. It is now possible, for instance, for the church or the planning group to decide to major on the gospel story for the whole year, and to ensure that the preaching covers the retelling of the story in a way that is relevant to today. It is equally possible to major on the Old Testament or on the epistle for several weeks: a glance at the lectionary will show the length of time for which this can easily be done.

It is important that there is discussion with those who are preaching to understand from them the kind of line they are taking with a particular passage of Scripture, so that hymns may be chosen, particularly just before or after the sermon which will reinforce rather than conflict with their theme.

It works best to major on one reading. But then that raises a question about how to handle the other readings. Are there going to be two or only one? Care must be taken not to highlight accidentally the reading which is not going to be the major one, for example leaving the preacher struggling to continue his exposition of the argument of 2 Corinthians 6 after a riotous youth group dramatic presentation of David and Goliath (Proper 7, Year 2).

Reading all the readings for this particular Sunday, but focusing on the one on which the preacher is going to major on, may indicate particular hymns or items in the worship which may be suitable. Have regard to any particular seasonal emphasis. At some seasons it may help to tie the Sundays of the season together, for example by a repeated song or versicle and response or in Advent by the lighting of candles.

Liase with others who may have a creative input into this particular service, especially if they are not part of the planning group. This may include those with musical expertise, people in Sunday School, young peoples' groups who may be willing to take part, those with an interest in drama or dance and so on.

What kind of service is it? If it is a standard service for which the structure is already largely laid down, such as Morning or Evening Prayer or the Holy Communion, then you will need to discuss how the readings may be interpreted, for example through drama or a dramatic reading, or through some introductory word of explanation. There may be other items to add in, and certainly it will be necessary to look at the form and shape of the intercessions, to ensure that these reflect some of what is there in the lectionary readings. If the service is a Family Service or *A Service of the Word*, is it intended to use an outline which has already been prepared, such as the sample services in *Patterns for Worship*, or one which the church has agreed to use for the moment? Is the service going to lead into the

Holy Communion? If so, there will need to be a gospel reading, and there is a recognized order in which things need to be done, set out in *Patterns for Worship* on page 19.

If the service is being constructed from scratch, then the advice in the chapter on *A Service of the Word* in *Patterns for Worship* (page 13 and following) is very valuable. *A Service of the Word* provides the basic structure, with a beginning and an end and the Ministry of the Word, the Prayers and Praise. These 'building blocks' may be repeated more than once in the main body of the service.

It may be worth looking at other resource material, such as that provided in the books by Susan Sayers, or in the dated magazine material from the National Society or Scripture Union, or the new volume *Worship Through the Christian Year* which Church House Publishing are bringing out.

Once the outline of the service is complete, check it with the guidelines in *Patterns for Worship* (page 25).

It would be an interesting exercise to lay it out with the new lectionary readings at one side, and to draw lines between the readings and those parts of the service which they have influenced or which are directly related to them. This provides a useful check about how well the service is integrated. Decide how many of these links should be explicitly pointed out by those who lead the service—though not too many or it will be boring!

Review the number of people taking part in the service: Guideline 8 in *Patterns for Worship* says 'Does the service enable the gifts of a variety of people in the church to be used in both planning and taking part?' This can easily be checked by putting names against the various items on the list. It should be clear who is in overall charge and responsible for leading the worship, but that person should not attempt to do everything. A variety of voices and approaches is a good thing, providing it does not detract from the unity of the worship. Care needs to be given particularly to the readings. It may well be better to have a smaller number of people responsible for reading these well, rather than to involve a very wide range of people, some of whom may not be able to read very well. This applies particularly to Family Services and the temptation to get children to do too much. One way of helping people to see the relationship between the readings from one week to the next might be to have the same person reading say the Epistle or the Gospel for a number of weeks.

As you review the contents of the service, ask the question, 'What do we expect people to take away from this service, and what action do we expect them to take?' This should at least sharpen up the praying for those responsible for the worship, and encourage you to leave the outcome in the hands of the Holy Spirit!

Lastly, when the service has happened, the group or person responsible for planning it should spend some time reviewing how it went, how well related the material was to the readings, and what the overall effect was.

5
Hymns and the New Lectionary
Peter Moger

Introduction

The power of hymnody is widely acknowledged. The sung word often lodges far more deeply in the consciousness than does the spoken word. Hence, hymns are potent agents in shaping theology and spirituality. The right hymns—chosen with care and sensitivity to the flow of a service and to its scriptural content—can strengthen faith and enable worship. The wrong hymns can wreck both.

This chapter will deal mainly with hymns and psalms, but of course many churches enjoy a mixed diet of traditional hymns and worship songs, and similar principles apply to the selection of both. While some longer songs might be classified as hymns (in that they contain extended reflection upon a theological theme), most are of a different order altogether. John Leach's powerfully argued thesis, that hymns and songs are the product of separate cultures, is to be taken seriously (if not swallowed whole).[17] The assumption that hymns and songs are interchangeable in any liturgical context should be challenged—a worship song will sometimes work far better than a traditional hymn—and an approach to the use of both, that does justice to a church's prevailing worship culture, must be explored.

A Change of Approach

Since 1980, choosing hymns for Anglican worship has been a relatively straightforward affair. The *ASB* Sunday lectionary is organized according to theme and, in the main, hymns have been selected to reflect Sunday themes—aiming to bind together readings, music and preaching in a unified whole. The appendices in the major hymnals have encouraged this, providing lists of suggested hymns to fit the *ASB* themes.[18]

There are problems with this approach. First, it can encourage hymn choice on 'auto-pilot.' Clergy and musicians—pressed for time—can opt for the four or five most popular hymns from the lists provided, sometimes without sufficient regard for their appropriate place within the liturgy. Second, the 'Sunday theme' approach has enabled choices to be made without the necessity of studying the appointed Scripture passages—a danger which also exists for preachers. Third, it has in many cases restricted the size of the base from which hymns have been chosen. Despite the growing ease of legal copying through CCL and Calamus schemes, there is evidence that many congregations exist on a severely restricted

---

17 John Leach. *Hymns and Spiritual Songs: The Use of Traditional and Modern in Worship* (Grove Worship Series No 132. Nottingham: Grove Books. 1995).
18 *The New English Hymnal, Hymns Ancient and Modern New Standard, Hymns for Today's Church.* See also David Barker. *The Hymns and Songs List* (Hodder and Stoughton. 1992).

diet of hymns, often repeated on an annual cycle.

The new lectionary sees the disappearance of Sunday themes. Those who choose hymns will need to ask some searching liturgical questions and take time to engage more directly with the biblical text.

Taking the Seasons Seriously

Human beings are seasonal creatures and a clearly articulated structure to the year is an important given in a world where so much is perpetually shifting. The new calendar provides this structure and it is crucial that music works with the calendar and not against it. Clergy and musicians will need to be clear in their own minds about the thinking behind the calendar, and have the courage to challenge some of the assumptions they encounter.

Other contributors have written in greater detail about the composition of the new calendar. Of crucial importance is that Sundays are 'of' a particular season, not 'after' a Festival. Each season is thus a unity—for example Epiphany, which runs from 6 January until 2 February (and thus, taken with Christmas, forms a block of 40 days). The implication for hymnody is considerable—hymns about the incarnation are in many cases suitable throughout the whole season. For instance, a highly appropriate hymn for 2 February—to round off the season—is *Angels from the Realms of Glory*,[19] since it links the nativity, the shepherds, the wise men and the presentation. It is sad that we have colluded with secular culture in ceasing to sing Christmas hymns before the season has really got underway in the New Year. It will need strength to counter this prevailing mentality, but the result will be the considerable enrichment of our worship.

The Epiphany season also draws on the theological connection of Baptism, Trinity and Kingdom, a link not explicit in the *ASB* scheme. Other seasonal nuances which need to be communicated through hymnody are the change of mood part way through Advent (17 December: when the antiphon *O Sapientia* begins the eight days of prayer before Christmas Day), and the nine days of prayer before Pentecost. Here there is a challenge to create—through hymnody—an atmosphere of waiting: for the birth of Christ; for the gift of the Spirit. Many traditional Pentecost hymns are in fact invocations of the Spirit,[20] and these might usefully be sung in the run up to Pentecost. The Feast of Christ the King (the Sunday next before Advent), offers a new opportunity to sing many of the hymns currently associated with Ascensiontide.[21] The new calendar means that we shall often have to reassess the principles behind our choice of hymns, and to be clear about why we are singing what we sing.

---

19 AMNS 39.
20 For example *Holy Spirit, come confirm us* (NEH 140). *Come down, O Love Divine* (NEH 137). *Come, thou Holy Spirit, come* (NEH 139). *Breathe on me, breath of God* (NEH 342).
21 For example *Crown him with many crowns* (NEH 352). *Christ triumphant* (HTC 173). *All hail the power of Jesus' name* (NEH 332).

Taking Scripture Seriously

The new lectionary presents its greatest challenge for hymnody, though, through its approach to Scripture. The contrast with the *ASB* scheme is seen most clearly in the provision for Ordinary Time, when the readings are not governed by seasonal considerations. In Year A of the Principal Service lectionary, for instance, the lections run through consecutive passages from Genesis, Romans and Matthew. The hymns would need to take account of this, and be selected for the way in which they illuminate or reflect upon the texts—texts which are not held together by a common theme.

Anglican hymnals are not renowned for exhaustive scriptural indices. *The New English Hymnal* and *Hymns Ancient and Modern New Standard* provide no such index, and that in *Hymns for Today's Church* is hardly comprehensive and compares poorly with that in *Hymns and Psalms*.[22] A valuable existing resource is Michael Perry's *Preparing for Worship*[23] which lists hymns and songs against biblical references (chapter and verse). A forthcoming publication which promises to be excellent is *Sing his Glory: Hymns for the New Lectionary, Years A, B and C*.[24] The editors have adopted the principle of selecting hymns which reflect upon the readings of the Principal Service with choices made from nine major hymnals.[25] What this new guide does not attempt to do is dictate *where* in a service a particular hymn should be sung. That, as the editors remark, 'is a matter of liturgy rather than lectionary.'[26]

Taking the Liturgy Seriously

Ever since I was once asked to sing
> 'Strengthen for service, Lord, the hands
> that holy things have taken'

as a Gradual hymn, I have become passionately concerned about the role of hymns within the liturgy, and of the importance of their correct placing. When putting together any service, we should ask two questions of each hymn: (1) 'What job are we expecting it to do?' and (2) 'How does it fit the shape and flow of the liturgy?' Eucharistic liturgy, in particular, has an in-built sense of flow. Hymnody should support and enhance this and not, as is often the case, run counter to it.

A 'traditional' Rite A Parish Communion might include five hymns:

1. An opening hymn (which might cover a procession of clergy and/or a choir),
2. A Gradual hymn before the gospel,
3. A hymn at the preparation of the gifts ('Offertory'),
4. A hymn during the administration and
5. A post-communion hymn.

---

22 Methodist Publishing House, 1983.   23 Marshall Pickering, 1995.
24 Canterbury Press, November 1997. £8.99.
25 *Hymns Ancient and Modern New Standard, The New English Hymnal, Hymns for Today's Church, Hymns Old and New (Anglican), Mission Praise (Combined), Hymns and Psalms, Rejoice and Sing, Baptist Praise and Worship, The Church Hymnary (3rd edition)*.
26 Preface to *Sing his Glory, op cit.*

Each of these has a clearly defined liturgical function and it is crucial that this is understood and that the choice of each is appropriate. An opening hymn should, above all, gather the congregation in worship and set the tone for the service. On a feast day or in a clearly defined season it might be thematic. It is always helpful if such a hymn is well-known. If there is processional movement or ceremonial action during a gathering hymn, the hymn should be long enough to cover this.[27]

A good Gradual hymn will aim to focus on the readings or on the person of Christ as presented in the gospel reading. Brevity is a virtue here, though never at the expense of good theology.[28] Fine hymns on Scripture are rare. Most mainstream hymnals contain a few of these, but it is sometimes necessary to supplement from another source. An excellent selection can be found amongst hymns appointed for the Office of Readings in *Hymns for Prayer and Praise*.[29]

An 'Offertory' hymn should be long enough to cover the presentation and preparation of the gifts, but its liturgical purpose is to effect the gear-change from word and prayer to sacrament.[30] It need not, though, have an explicitly eucharistic focus. Coming before the *Sursum Corda*, this hymn can be a powerful means of exhorting the congregation to 'lift up their hearts' and to prepare to become part of the worship of 'the whole company of heaven.' A good many 'general hymns' of praise work well at this point in the liturgy.

The best hymns for singing during the administration are those that are devotional within a eucharistic frame of reference. The administration, and not the offertory, is often the best place for hymns which focus on Christ's sacrifice and his presence in the Communion, though enormous care needs to be taken at this point in the liturgy. Even the right hymn played too noisily can seriously destroy a worshipful atmosphere. Alternative to traditional hymnody here (worship songs, Taizé chants or instrumental music) are often preferable.

A final hymn should complement the post-communion liturgy in that is should send out the people of God 'to live and work to his praise and glory.' The most appropriate position for such a hymn is between a post-communion prayer and the blessing,[31] not as a recessional hymn. Without the need to cover movement, a post-communion hymn need not be long.[32]

At some services (Services of the Word, Mattins, Evensong and 1662 Communion), the shape of the liturgy allows for a hymn to be sung after the sermon. This provides a golden opportunity to draw together threads from Scripture and the theme of the sermon, and to enable the congregation to respond in words which 'own' the thoughts that have been expressed. Care needs to be taken that

---

27 If an organ improvisation is needed for 'filling in' during ceremonial, such an improvisation should almost always come before the final verse of the hymn and not at the end.
28 An example of an excellent longer Gradual hymn might be *The sinless one to Jordan came* (*NEH* 58) for the Feast of the Baptism of Christ (First Sunday of Epiphany, *RCL*).
29 Canterbury Press for the Panel of Monastic Musicians, 1996.
30 An obvious example for Ascensiontide is *Alleluia, sing to Jesus*.
31 This is the position envisaged in Rites A and B revised.
32 A superb example of a post-communion hymn is Charles Wesley's *Glory, love and praise and honour* (*NEH* 287).

(unless it is the final hymn in a service) a post-sermon hymn does not 'send out' the congregation too soon, and that it does not contradict the preacher's message!

Psalms

The new lectionary provides psalms for use at principal, second and third services. Anglicanism has always placed a high value on psalmody and it is vital that psalms are not lost from (especially) eucharistic Sunday worship. In Rites A and B Revised, it is envisaged that a psalm (or canticle) 'follows the first reading.'[33] Hence, if the custom is to have three readings, a psalm may be used between the first and second, or, if there are two, as a Gradual before the gospel. The many ways psalms may effectively be sung in modern worship is an extensive subject beyond the scope of this booklet—but one worth exploring afresh for each congregation.[34] *Sing his Glory* suggests metrical psalm settings where these are readily available, and in the absence of a suitable metrical setting, selects hymns which try to draw out the message of the appointed psalm.

Planning

The need for careful planning of hymnody is crucial. Planning is best done well in advance and, ideally, for a period of several months at a time, thus cutting out the likelihood of over-repetition. It is certainly worth planning each season of the Church's year at one sitting in order to ensure cohesion and a clear sense of direction.

Hymn selection is a balancing act. Within the constraints of season, theme and liturgical framework, hymns should be chosen which display variety in metre and provenance. To sing too many hymns of like metre in one service makes for boredom, as does to sing hymns from only one century. Where it is known that there will be a visiting preacher, his/her suggestions about hymns should be sought well in advance, though Canon B20 might need to be invoked on occasion!

Over a period of time, new items can (and should) be introduced alongside those already in repertoire. New hymns, though, need to be carefully placed. A service at which the congregation is composed largely of visitors is not a good occasion to introduce new material, nor is (usually) an opening hymn. It is always worth rehearsing a new hymn beforehand and, if possible, printing the melody on a service sheet (though care needs to be taken not to infringe copyright here).

It is also important to keep a record of the hymns that are sung—partly to avoid needless repetition, and to counter the inevitable comment that 'we never sing *Summer suns are glowing* any more'!

---

33 *Holy Communion Rites A & B Revised—Report to the General Synod July 1996*, (General Synod, 1996) pp 16, 29.
34 A culture which supposes that Anglican chant is the only 'proper' medium for psalm-singing is decidedly difficult to break, but the fact remains that there are very few parishes which have the resources to sing Anglican chant well.